First Printing: 2018

ISBN 978-1-387-88758-3

Axe Credit Solutions
wwwAxeCreditCare.com

Disclaimer

The information contained in this book and its components are meant to serve as a comprehensive collection of strategies that the author of this book has done research about. Summaries, strategies, tips, and tricks are only recommendations by the author, and reading this book will not guarantee that one's results will exactly mirror the author's results or those implied.

The author of this book has made all reasonable efforts to provide current and accurate information for the readers of this book. The author and its associates will not be held liable for any unintentional errors or omissions that may be found. Whether because of the progression of the Internet, unforeseen changes in company policy, law changes, and/or editorial submission guidelines, what is stated at the time of this writing may become outdated or inapplicable later.

The material in the book may include information by third parties. Third party materials comprise of opinions expressed by their owners. As such, the author of this book does not assume responsibility or liability for any third-party material or opinions.

CONTENTS

Chapter ONE 6

CREDIT REPAIR...6

WHAT IS A CREDIT SCORE? 6

WHAT'S ON MY CREDIT PROFILE? 7

WHAT IS CREDIT REPAIR? 9

HOW LONG DOES IT TAKE?...10

HOW DOES IT WORK?...11

IS IT LEGAL?..11

Chapter TWO 13

THE BUREAUS...13

EQUIFAX, TRANSUNION, EXPERIAN 13

CREDIT LAWS YOU NEED TO KNOW 14

FAIR DEBT COLLECTION PRACTICES ACT 14

MYTHS VS FACTS..16

Chapter THREE 19

TYPES OF CREDIT...19

CREDIT MIX 19

SCORE CALCULATION- HOW IS MY CREDIT SCORE CALCULATED? 20

WHAT TO DISPUTE 21

Chapter FOUR 22

CREDIT REPAIR GUIDE...22

CHECK CHALLENGE CHANGE...22

Chapter FIVE...**25**

BEYOND CREDIT REPAIR..25

CREDIT TIPS...25

BEWARE: PEOPLE/COMPANIES THAT SAY THIS…................27

Credit Care Tracker **31**

DISPUTE LETTERS..33

BASIC DISPUTE LETTER TO CREDIT BUREAU........................33

MULTIPLE REQUESTS...34

ESCALATED DISPUTE LETTER...35

DEBT VALIDATION FORM 37

REQUEST FOR REMOVAL OF INCORRECT INFORMATION BY CREDITOR.......38

REQUEST TO DESCRIBE INVESTIGATION PROCESS 39

"PROVE IT" DISPUTE LETTER 40

VERIFICATION OF METHOD 41

VALIDATION OF MEDICAL DEBT FROM CREDITOR.................42

ACCOUNT REMOVAL DUE TO FRAUD....................................43

INQUIRY REMOVAL...44

Industry Contacts..**45**

Chapter ONE

CREDIT REPAIR

Let's face it, there is virtually nothing today that you can't do yourself. Credit Repair included! You can fix your car, represent yourself in court, etc. and credit repair is no exception. Leverage your legal rights to investigate, dispute, and challenge negative items on your credit report. All you need are the right tools, information, and guidance and you will be on your way to increasing your credit score and improving your financial life.

What is a Credit Score?

A credit score is the number that paints a picture of how trustworthy you are to lenders. For example, the higher the number, the more trustworthy you appear to be, which equates as a low risk to the lender. The lower the number, the more of a risk you appear to be in repaying back what was borrowed. Regardless if you are applying for a car loan, home loan, business loan, or personal loan, lenders will want to determine your level of credit.

What's on My Credit Profile?

Your credit profile is your personal resume. It tells a story of your financial decisions. The three reporting agencies are Equifax, Experian, and TransUnion. Although they all report differently, they report the same categories of information.

Personal Information:

Your names used (current and past), social security number, and employment information (current and past). This information has no bearing on your actual credit score, but still should be accurate.

Trade Lines:

The accounts you have (current and past). Virtually anything that requires an amount (credit cards, loans, etc.). Also, shown in this section is the date opened, amount or credit limit, and payment history.

Inquiries:

Every time you apply for a loan, you are giving authorization to the lender to request a copy of your credit report. This is an inquiry and shows on your credit report. Inquiries last up to two years and make a negative impact on your credit. Inquiries can be both voluntary and involuntary.

Collections and Public Records:

The credit bureaus also collect public information from state and county court systems. Public records include bankruptcies, lawsuits, wage garnishments, foreclosures, judgments, and liens.

What is Credit Repair?

Credit repair is a process in which you are notifying the credit bureaus and/or creditors of items on your credit profile that are incorrect by disputing the validity. These items typically have impacted your credit score in a negative way, and therefore when disputing, you must state the nature of the dispute. Credit repair could be as simple as disputing these mistakes or may require extensive credit repair for situations such as identity theft. But credit repair doesn't stop there. It also includes the fundamentals of financial literacy in budgeting and credit appropriation.

How Long Does It Take?

Not two credit profiles are alike, and therefore everyone's timeline will be different. The amount of time depends on the number of derogatory items on your credit profile, staying on top of the response timelines, and the level of cooperation from the credit bureaus and creditors. By law, the credit bureaus and creditors have 30-45 days to respond to each round of disputes. That is where majority of the time is taking place. Hurrying up to wait! The credit bureaus are required by law to respond to each correspondence sent to them. With that being said, it is not uncommon for the credit bureaus to respond wanting more information or not wanting to re-verify an account. Often times, they won't respond at all. Just like you will have a dispute tactic, so do the credit bureaus and creditors. REMEMBER: They profit from your bad credit!

How Does It Work?

Credit disputes can be filed if you see any incomplete or inaccurate information on your credit profile. In addition to correcting such information and potentially catching fraudulent activity, repairing your credit does rely heavily on your credit usage and activity as well.   By law, if the credit bureaus can't verify the information being disputed, the item MUST be removed from your credit profile.

Is It Legal?

Absolutely! I always say it's one of the few times the law is actually on the consumer's side! The Fair Credit Reporting Act is in place and gives consumers the right to dispute anything they believe to be incorrect and inaccurate.   Any inaccurate, outdated, incomplete, and/or unverifiable information or accounts must be removed or corrected. Although credit repair companies are regulated, anything a credit repair company can do, you can do yourself if you have the time and patience. It could save you hundreds, even thousands to repair your credit yourself.

Chapter TWO

THE BUREAUS

Equifax, TransUnion, Experian

Why are there three different credit bureaus? From getting approved for a credit card to getting the lowest interest rates on a mortgage or car loan, Equifax, Experian, and TransUnion are the gatekeepers to the types of offers you receive.

It may surprise you, but the credit bureaus are NOT government agencies! In fact, they have absolutely no government affiliation at all. All three of them are private companies that collect your information from creditors. Information such as financial history, behavior that come from banks, lenders, credit card companies, cell phone providers, utility companies, and healthcare providers. What that means is, they profit from your bad credit!

The information varies from bureau to bureau due to the information provided being a voluntary process from the creditor. This is why you have three completely different scores. Not only is the data different, the scoring methods are also. When you're ready to see what is on your credit profile from all three bureaus, you are entitled to one free credit report (every 12 months) from AnnualCreditReport.com.

Credit Laws You Need to Know

Take a deep breath. There are actually plenty of credit laws that can come to your rescue. Most of these credit laws have been around since 1970 and can give you some serious credit power. The Fair Debt Collection Practices Act (FDCPA), for example, prohibits debt collectors from calling you 24/7, whereas the Fair Credit Reporting Act (FCRA) is meant to guarantee accuracy on your credit report.

Fair Debt Collection Practices Act

Gives you the right to ask the collection agency to verify your debt. By law, the collectors have to stop collecting if you dispute the collection in question. If found inaccurate or if the item can't be verified, you can remove inaccurate, erroneous and obsolete items such as late payments, charge-offs, foreclosures, judgments, repossessions, bankruptcies, tax liens, collections, short sales, and medical bills.

Fair Credit Reporting Act

The FCRA is a federal law that is in place to regulate credit reporting agencies and how they report information. The law is intended to ensure accuracy of information on the consumer's credit history and to protect the consumer against misinformation being used against him.

State Statute of Limitations

Every state has a statute of limitations for debts which vary by state. They're typically between 3 to 6 years from the time when you fell behind on a debt, or from the date of your last payment. By law, a debt collector cannot collect on a debt that falls out of the statute of limitations.

Myths vs Facts

Myth #1

Credit Agencies have some form of governmental authority?

Fact: Credit agencies have no legal authority and are not government agencies. They are private companies who are in the business of selling credit information and profiting off your bad credit.

Myth #2

All three credit bureaus are required by law to keep derogatory items on your credit report for up to 7 to 10 years?

Fact: No law states the requirement to report any information on you at all. The credit bureaus are, however, required by law to automatically remove most derogatory items older than seven years (in some cases 10 years).

Myth #3

You cannot change the information on your credit report; in fact, it is illegal or immoral to do so?

Fact: Under the Fair Credit Reporting Act, the items must be removed if they are not 100% accurate and/or cannot be verified in a timely manner.

Myth #4

Paying a debt automatically removes it from your credit report?

Fact: No. Paying the debt doesn't change the fact that at one time you were delinquent. However, asking for a deletion upon payment will remove the item.

Myth #5

Inquiries will not affect your credit score?

Fact: Inquires tell a story of your financial decisions, needs, and wants. Having a few is not bad, however an excess amount gives the impression you are applying for too much credit and/or getting denied.

Chapter THREE

TYPES OF CREDIT

Credit Mix

Believe it or not, having a diverse credit profile actually helps you. Your credit mix makes up 10% of your credit score calculation. Many lenders favor consumers who can handle different types of credit well. If you want the top credit score, you know the one that gets you the best rates and highest credit limits, you're going to have to mix it up a bit. In fact, FICO's research found that with all things being equal, consumers with a mix of credit on their credit profile tend to be less risky. Here are the types of credit:

- Installment loans, including auto loans, student loans and furniture purchases

- Mortgage loans

- Bank credit cards

- Retail credit cards

- Gas station credit cards

- Rental data

Keep in mind this information is more of a "good to know" rather than "I need to go apply in different credit categories." Always put paying onetime and low balances as a priority.

Score Calculation- How is my credit score calculated?

Your FICO score is made from Fair Isaac and they are adamant about not sharing how they calculate your credit score. However, what they do give is information on the categories that are used to calculate your score and the weight they have. Credit score range from 300-850, with anything over 740 being considered excellent credit and anything below a 640 being fair. Below is the makeup of what is used to calculate your credit score.

- ➢ 35% payment history
- ➢ 30% amount owed
- ➢ 15% length of history
- ➢ 10% new credit
- ➢ 10% types of credit used

What to Dispute

By law, you can dispute anything on your credit profile that you believe to be inaccurate or erroneous. You can even report accurate information, but only if it is reporting multiple times on your credit profile. You will see that in the sample letters, the key is to have the information verified that it is indeed your account.

Tip: When your account is bought by a collection agency, the entire contents of the file aren't transferred, therefore, most of the time the account cannot be verified properly.

Chapter FOUR

Credit Repair Guide

Check Challenge Change

It is important to remember that this process may take a few rounds of disputes, which could mean as little as a few months to a year. What that means is, your first dispute letter may not remove all the items you have requested to be removed. That is ok, it is perfectly normal in the credit repair process. Everyone's credit profile is not the same, so don't compare process times. Just get started!

Step 1: Pull your credit report. You need to get a copy of all three of your credit files from Equifax, TransUnion, and Experian. Most free third-party credit monitoring companies only give you just one or two of them.

Step 2: Review your reports for errors or items you deemed to be incorrect and as a result has a negative credit report.

Step 3: List the items in question in your pre-filled dispute letters. Attach a copy of your Driver's License and Social Security card and send the letter via USPS to all three credit bureaus. So, that's three envelopes. You have the option of sending them certified for better tracking.

Step 4: Wait for a response (within 30-45 days) while the creditor and/or bureau investigates. You should get an update from the credit bureaus by mail. The update will list any changes made and to what accounts.

Step 5: Update your credit repair log located in the back of this book. Remove, respond, repeat

Chapter FIVE

BEYOND CREDIT REPAIR

Credit repair isn't just about permanently deleting incorrect negative items off your credit profile. It's about changing your whole mindset and the way you view finances so that you don't get to this place again. And when life happens, you already know the tricks of the trade on how to avoid missed payments, delinquencies, collections, and just overall bad credit. Here are some credit tips to help you.

Credit Tips

➢ 30% of your credit score is based on your debt. Once you have increased your credit score, ask for a credit limit increase from your credit card company. This can be done online.

➢ **Avoid closing your oldest accounts. Even if you don't use them anymore. The longer the history you have reporting (positive of course!), the better your score will be.**

- By becoming an authorized user on a trusted friend or family member's credit card account, your credit profile is getting the history from that account. This will only work if you don't have an excess amount of late payments or collection accounts. IMPORTANT: the account must be in good standing, preferably with zero to low balance and the older the account, the better.

- **Before you miss a payment, contact the company and try to work out an additional grace period. You'd be surprised how willing they are to work with you.**

- Do not pay a debt in collections. I repeat don't pay anything in collections! Once the original creditor has sold your debt, they forfeited the right to collect any money!

- **Pay half of your credit card payment <u>15 days before</u> the due date. Then pay the remaining half <u>3 days before</u> the due date. You trick the system into thinking you've made two FULL payments.**

- Up to two years of your rental history can and should be reported on your credit profile to help increase your credit score. Get credit for paying rent!

> **NEVER dispute online! When you do that, you waive your right to see the method of verification received by the credit bureaus.**

Beware: People/Companies that say this…

Let's face it, everyone is in the credit repair business nowadays. Kudos to them! I love to see people not only in business but helping others as well. With that said, there are a lot of scammers and individuals that claim their credit repair services are an easy quick process. I've even heard, "Erase everything and even get another social security number!" Those are very dangerous words. In fact, the credit repair industry is heavily regulated by the Federal Trade Commission. If you hear any of these comments or phrases from a company or individual, RUN the other way!

> We guarantee an increase in your credit score, or your money back
> Asks you to file a police report or identity theft report
> Tells you to not contact the credit report agencies
> You can erase everything off your credit report

- It'll only take 30 days (or any specified timeframe) to fix your credit

- If they pressure you to pay up-front fees

- Refuses or avoids explaining your rights

- Implies guarantee loan approval

Now that you have the tools to repair and increase your credit score, it's time to get started. Go back a few pages, follow the step by step instructions, use the credit care tracker, and wait to see "Congratulations, your credit score has increased!"

Credit Care Tracker

Axe Credit Solutions *Credit Care Tracker*

Items Desputed	Debt Amount	Bureau/ Creditor	Date Sent	Outcome/Notes
Example: Capital One	$3,252	Experian	1/1/2018	Responded 2/15/18, Deleted
		TransUnion	1/1/2018	Responded 2/15/18, Deleted

Axe Credit Solutions *Credit Care Tracker*

Items Desputed	Debt Amount	Bureau/ Creditor	Date Sent	Outcome/Notes
Example: Capital One	$3,252	Experian	1/1/2018	Responded 2/15/18, Deleted
		TransUnion	1/1/2018	Responded 2/15/18, Deleted

Axe Credit Solutions *Credit Care Tracker*

Items Desputed	Debt Amount	Bureau/ Creditor	Date Sent	Outcome/Notes
Example: Capital One	$3,252	Experian	1/1/2018	Responded 2/15/18, Deleted
		TransUnion	1/1/2018	Responded 2/15/18, Deleted

DISPUTE LETTERS

Basic Dispute Letter to Credit Bureau

Name
Address

Credit Bureau
Address

Date

Dear Credit Bureau,

Upon reviewing my credit report for inaccuracies, I noticed there are still several accounts on my credit file that are not correct and for that reason **I am requesting validation pursuant to the Fair Debt Collection Practices Act, 15 USC 1692g Sec. 809 (8) (FDCPA), I have the right to request validation of the debt you say I owe. I am also requesting proof that I am indeed the party you are asking to pay this debt, and there is some contractual obligation which is binding on me to pay this debt.**

Please remove the following below if you can't provide any debt validation:

1. List Collection Accounts & Account Numbers

Please remove the accounts from my credit report. Once the accounts have been removed, please send me an updated credit report reflecting the changes.

Thank you,

Name

Multiple Requests

Name

Address

Credit Bureau

Address

Date

Dear Credit Bureau,

This is the second/ third letter I am sending to you demanding an investigation on inaccuracies remaining in my credit file. The most recent letter was sent over thirty days ago with no response from your company to date. I am very dissatisfied with the lack of service I have received and demand that you reinvestigate the accounts listed below:

Accounts	**Reason**
• List Collection Accounts	ex. This is not my account

As stated previously I have maintained a log of all my letter sent to your company. If you do not respond immediately to this request, I will have no other choice but to contact the FTC or a similar regulatory agency. Your prompt response is required.

Thank you,
Name

Escalated Dispute Letter

Name

Address

Credit Bureau or Creditor

Address

Date

To Whom It May Concern:

Pursuant to the Fair Debt Collection Practices Act, 15 USC 1692g Sec. 809 (8) (FDCPA), I have the right to request validation of the debt you say I owe you. I am requesting proof that I am indeed the party you are asking to pay this debt, and there is some contractual obligation which is binding on me to pay the following items:

1. List Collection Accounts & Account Numbers

In addition to the questionnaire below, please attach copies of ALL of the following:

- o Agreement with your client that grants you the authority to collect on this alleged debt, or proof of acquisition by purchase or assignment.
- o Agreement that bears the signature of the alleged debtor wherein he or she agreed to pay the creditor.
- o Please evidence your authorization under 15 USC 1692(e) and 15 USC 1692(f) in this alleged matter.
- o What is your authorization of law for your collection of information?
- o What is your authorization of law for your collection of this alleged debt?
- o Please evidence your authorization to do business or operate in this state.
- o Please evidence proof of the alleged debt, including the alleged contract or another instrument bearing my signature.

- Please provide a complete account history, including any charges added for collection activity.

Also, please be advised this letter is not only a formal dispute, but a request for you to cease and desist any and all collection activities. I require compliance with the terms and conditions of this letter within 30 days. or a complete withdrawal, in writing, of any claim.

In the event of noncompliance, I reserve the right to file charges and/or complaints with appropriate County, State & Federal authorities the BBB and State Bar associations for violations of the FDCPA, FCRA, and Federal and State statutes on fraudulent extortion.

Sincerely,
Name

Debt Validation Form

Please provide all of the following information and submit the appropriate forms and paperwork within 30 days from the date of your receipt of this request for validation.

Alleged Full Account #: _____

Original Creditor's Name:_____

Name of Debtor:_____

Address of Debtor:_____

Balance of Account:_____

Date you purchased this debt:_____

Date of original charge off or delinquency:_____

Amount paid if debt was purchased:_____

Commission for debt collector if successful:_____

This Debt was: assigned _____ purchased_____

Please indicate the credit bureaus which you have reported this account to:
Experian: _____ Equifax: _____ TransUnion: _____

Thank you!

Name

Request for Removal of Incorrect Information by Creditor

Name
Address

Creditor
Address

Date

To Whom It May Concern:

On (Date), I received a copy of my credit history report from (Credit Bureau Name). The report contained incorrect information reported by you.

I contacted the (Credit Bureau Name) to request deletion of this inaccurate data, but they have refused. They insist that your company claims this information to be accurately reported. This is not true. Please remove the following:

- List account information

This negative mark is damaging to my credit. Please contact Experian, Equifax, and TransUnion immediately to remove this information from my credit file.

Please confirm to me within 20 days that you have contacted the credit bureaus to correct this information.

Thank you
Name

Request to Describe Investigation Process

Name
Address

Creditor
Address

Date

To Whom It May Concern:

This letter is a formal request for the description of the procedures used to determine the accuracy and completeness of the disputed information, including business name, address, and telephone number of any furnisher of information contacted in connection with this reinvestigation.

- List Collection Accounts

I am disappointed that you have failed to maintain reasonable procedures to assure complete accuracy in the information you publish, and insist you comply with the law by providing the requested information within the 15 days allowed.

As already stated, the listed items are inaccurate and is a very serious error in reporting. Please provide the name, address, and telephone number of each credit grantor or another subscriber.

Thank you
Name

"Prove it" Dispute Letter

Name
Address

Creditor
Address

Date

To Whom It May Concern:

I am in disagreement with the items listed below, which still appear on my credit report, even after your investigation. I would like these items immediately re-investigated as these items are highly injurious to my credit score.

- List Collection Accounts

Furthermore, in accordance with The Fair Credit Reporting Act, Public law 91-506, Title VI, Section 611, Subsection A-D, please provide the names and business addresses of each individual with whom you verified the above, so that I may follow up.

Please forward me an updated credit report with the completed corrections.

Thank you
Name

Verification of Method

Name
Address

Creditor
Address

Date

To Whom It May Concern:

I am writing to request the method of verification for dispute.

- List Collection Accounts

Please send the following information used to verify the validity of above listed accounts.

1. The name of the original creditor
2. The creditors address and telephone number
3. The person's name they verified the dispute with
4. The documentation used to verify the dispute

In accordance with FCRA, Section 611, I am requesting this information to review for completeness and accuracy and appropriateness. In lieu of sending the information you can reopen the dispute and ensure a proper investigation is performed.

I would appreciate a timely response outlining the steps that will occur to resolve this matter. If I do not receive a response, I will have no choice but to exercise my right under FRCA, Section 616, and pursue legal action.

Thank you

Name

Validation of Medical Debt from Creditor

Name
Address

Creditor
Address

Date

To Whom It May Concern:

I received a bill from you and as allowable under the Fair Debt Collection Practices Act, I am requesting a validation of the alleged debt. I am unaware of the debt and unaware of the detailed breakdown of any fees allegedly owed.

Furthermore, I am allowed under the HIPPA law to protect my privacy and medical records from third parties. I do not recall giving my permission to any third parties inquiring. Please provide the following:

- Validation of Debt
- HIPPA Authorization
- Breakdown of any fees including medical charges
- A copy of my signature releasing my information

Please cease any credit bureau reporting until this debt has been verified.

Please note, that withholding information received from medical providers will be in violation of HIPPA and FDCPA laws. Furthermore, any reporting of this debt to the credit bureaus prior to allowing me to validate it may be an additional violation, in which allows me the right to seek damages.

Thank you
Name

Account Removal Due to Fraud

Name
Address

Credit Bureau
Address

Date

Re: Incorrect reporting on my credit report

To whom it may concern:

I received a copy of my credit report and I am disputing the items that need to be deleted due to identity theft. I have listed the accounts below along with the dates they were opened and balances:

1. **List collection accounts & balance**

Please remove immediately

Please notify me that the above items have been deleted pursuant to §(a) (6) [usc u.s code §1861j (a) (6)]. In the event of noncompliance, I reserve the right to file charges and/or complaints with appropriate county, state & federal authorities the BBB and state bar associations for violations of the FDCPA, FCRA, and federal and state statutes.

Please attach the FTC affidavit to all disputes and remove these items due to identity theft. I am also requesting an updated copy of my credit report.

Sincerely,
Name

Inquiry Removal

Name
Address

Credit Bureau
Address

Date

Re: Unauthorized inquiry

To whom it may concern:

I reviewed a copy of my credit report & I noticed several unauthorized credit inquiries. Please see below the list of merchants and dates of the inquiries.

1. List inquiry and date

Please remove immediately

I never authorized these actions. Please notify me that the above items have been deleted pursuant to §(a) (6) [usc u.s code §1861j (a) (6)]. In the event of noncompliance, I reserve the right to file charges and/or complaints with appropriate county, state & federal authorities the BBB and state bar associations for violations of the FDCPA, FCRA, and federal and state statutes.

I am also requesting an updated copy of my credit report.

Sincerely,
Name

Industry Contacts

Consumer Credit Laws
www.FTC.gov

Fraud Reporting
www.IdentityTheft.gov

Credit Score Monitoring
www.PrivacyGuard.com

Free Yearly Credit Report
www.AnnualCreditReport.com

Equifax Information Services, LLC
P.O. Box 740256
Atlanta, GA 30374
www.Equifax.com

Experian
P.O. Box 9701
Allen, TX 75013
www.Experian.com

TransUnion LLC
P.O. Box 2000
Chester, PA 19022
www.TransUnion.com

38925617R00027

Made in the USA
San Bernardino, CA
15 June 2019